ORYGUN

ORYGUN

POEMS

BY **JESSICA TYNER**

OTHER BOOKS OF POETRY

The Last Exotic Petting Zoo, SMOOTH STONES PRESS 2014
What Makes an Always, SMOOTH STONES PRESS 2015

COPYRIGHT

Edited by Kermit Heartsong and Irina Kuzminsky
Cover Photographs courtesy Shutterstock
Cover Design: Wabi Sabi Design Group (WSDG)

For Chintan. "Orygun" was my first home. You are my last.

TABLE OF CONTENTS

ORYGUN

HOW TO KILL A LION

I was born a month late, hell bent
on breaking in as a Leo. I've always
done things on my own time. *Stubborn
as a bulldog*, my mom would say.
Bullheaded, raged a littering of exes
I left twirling in the wake. But pride
makes us do dumb things, careless
things, dangerous tests of fate
that end in "should have died's". Forget
being a Cancer—the nurturers,
the charitable ones, the summer children
scrabbling about in the sand. Show me
the fire, soak me in jealousy, give me
a burning love for the record books.

We're lions, and they'll all want us

for our hides, those coarse manes, the weapons
that glisten like jewels in our maw.
Being wanted
is a glorious thing—it feeds our prides
and licks at our egos, makes us purr
like tired, trusting kittens
as they hound us down, hunt us,
kill us for sport.

ARACHNOPHOBIA

When I was five, I fled through the screen door
to the horse range out back. There, my mother's
screams didn't carry, my father's crashes
into silence were paused.

Beyond the barn,
grazing grass stretched tapered fingers to the sun

and I disappeared into the weeds. As a child,

the uncut grass was tall as a castle and solid
as stone—but my patch,
the hidden one near the hay stacks,
was a bed of royalty, the stuff of morning cartoons
where no mother voice could reach or father
anger dare rumble. It was mine and, densely,

I trusted it completely. That day, with chubby leg
leaps into the pasture, I burst
like a dragonfly into my escape and straight
into the threads of a spider's web. At the time
she seemed a monster, clutching fat and tight
against my chest, her iridescent work a veil
over my head, draperies on my bare shins.
Yellow and black with a bulbous body and legs
like lightning, I don't recall the sting
or the taste of proteinaceous, but I remember
the horror. The freezing. The trespass of it all.

GLUTTONY

The cherries, the birds
got them all, gobbled them up—
spit down the pits
for the lawnmower to chew through.
I was six, and the blank fields
went on for acres. Each spring
the blossoms birthed, the fruits
got heavy and the birds
got fat, feasted
like winged gods.

SERPENTINE

When you're this thin, everything you swallow
is showcased in profile—a gluttonous sideshow
act. The snake girl who gulps shame down whole,
all swollen belly and groaning muscles. I have
nowhere to hide, no trick pockets for remorse
or safes for binges. Everything I am is on display,
every poor choice, each mistake. Like a serpent,
I'm demoted to the floor, crawling in filth
and tonguing at ankles. They're salty,
those ankle bones, with sweet notes
from sweat and earthy tones seasoned with
landscape dust. With distended belly, I can't
move fast like I should, slip between landmines
or blend in familiar to the noise. But in these moments,
when I'm all scales stretched and heavy loads,
I feel like something solid. Something real. Something
you or nobody can choose to ignore.

WHAT THE BODY REMEMBERS

I was trained to look at the chest when jabbing
and hooking to the face. It does more
than keep the chin down. It dehumanizes
the target—that's more important than reading
the fear or strategies in their eyes. There were times
I felt a vomer bone give beneath my fist, sucked
flecks of spittle that wasn't my own spraying like perfume
across my lips and yet
I never saw their face. The fighting days
are over, but the body never forgets. My knuckles
are woven with burst veins like cracked glass. I still
breathe with a rush through the teeth when I carry
heavy loads. And when I pass someone on the street
whose gaze crawls over me like hungry spiders
my eyes still shoot to their chest, nestling
the chin like a newborn into the fold and tensing
my stomach, my spirit, for the hit.

NIGHT BIRDS

When the insomnia punches
the liver and my mind's as light
as my bones, I crank the heat
and stand naked before the glass.
The disease is most inspiring
amidst the dark, when my skin
glows like a Chinese lantern
and the subcutaneous fat remnants
whisper along my muscles
like ornaments. Scattered in the streets
are regrets paired two by two, grabbing
each other tight and halting towards
hangovers and sticky thighs. But this,
this is when I'm most lovely—
when I see my shoulders as coracoids
and not splintered used up kindling.
When my ribs are strong and deadly
as an iron maiden, not a cage where every bar
is memorized in bruises along my back.
Find me
in the darkest hour and I'll show you
something so exquisite it breaks
and hides fast as a specter
in the excruciating light of dawn.

TO BREAK FAST

Life crept back into me like a child
slipping into the big bed in the middle of the night.
Slowly,
silently, so as not to disturb
the sleeping giants within. I was light
in a way famine never allowed,
lucid,
the bony fingers of dangerous dreams slinking
off my shrunken arms. Just as nightmares
aren't welcome when a girl spoons close
to her mother's sleeping body, as they're scared
into submission by her father's monstrous snores,
my desire to vanish lifted like a morning stretch,
dissipating with a yawn at the pink, dawning light.

CRAFTS WITH BLUNT EDGES

I cut you out, like those crooked paper dolls
or the gingerbread house walls
that never stuck no matter
how much icing or gobs of gum drops I used.
I slashed you away like all the others—
the ones I walked away from brisk
with a clip, no lingering
kisses or wondered what-ifs. It's always
been easy to leave, to turn my back
and trust that I alone
am enough to lift myself above the wreckage.

THE BUTCHERY DATE

I'm a dumb animal staring down the butcher
block. For a while, the stables feel like home, the cages
like comfort. We don't realize the burn
from the branding rod is forever, that the fire
burrows under seared flesh and scars straight
to spongy marrow. The prods move us forward,
calloused feet
shuffling toward the same bolt pistol ending
as everyone else. Fingernails and horns
are made from the same thing, tough envelopes
of keratin to ward off attacks. What's the difference
between locking horns in the bull rings and the slow
rides between unmade sheets? You'll find me
in the slaughter line of the abattoir—you'll know me
by your claw marks on my shoulder, the brute panic
in my eyes, that briny terror smell shooting from my pores
and because, well, of course,

we always knew we'd meet here.

GOOD MEDICINE

Today I wrote my fiftieth poem and it
was about you. Funny how that works,
how our histories sneak up on us
like boogeymen to the dreams of children.
I never wanted to be a doctor's
wife—it's a title bestowed upon
the damned like a king knighting a warrior
before sending him to glory-full death. I want
to make my own name, watch it grow
like a sea monkey with my words, not suffocate
with a stiffening smile beneath yours.
You saved my life long before your white
coats grew long to brush those swollen
thighs. For that I'm so grateful,
so on-my-knees, Jesus thankful
because you—you let me go.

MEN

There was the boy who asked, *How
do I know it's mine?* before I had the carelessness
vacuumed out. The one I left on impulse
after seven nothing years—who,
when I asked years later why
he didn't fight for me, said *I realized
you weren't worth fighting for.* Remember

the one who looked so damned good
at the bar in that across-the-room second—
the alcoholic I traded cries with, crumpled
in his medical scrubs? Then there was the man

whose dreadlocks whipped my arms raw, lucked
in with a visa lottery, he fed me sips of rum
on that first date 'round the mountain. His accent
was lovely, heady
and congealed but still,

he wasn't you. You usurped them all,
needled quick into my meat, the organs,
into the weight of my bones,
the buttery marrow of my body,

the everything of all I have to give.

FOR THE TITLE

I dried up all my fights fighting
for you, and I'm too tired,
too beaten,
too black and blue and busted
to do it anymore. I came back for that last round
(fighters always do) all split lip
and broken nose, bloodied knuckles
and dragging feet. Tell me,
did we make it through all the rounds? Did we
clinch tight enough, survive the rabbit
punches, and clean up real nice
from the dirty hooks and jabs? Listen,
you can hear the bells ring something sweet,
the crowds shuffle
toward the exits, feel the weight
of the gloves slip off our hands
while the judges huddle close—
all beady eyes and sorry bets.

THE L WORDS

I got up, still a little drunk, and ran
for miles after loving you. Sidewalks fell down,
verbs slammed against nouns, at four
in the morning I was leaving you.
My legs stretched 'til they broke, snapped
and tore with each stroke
and the sun—the sun
soaks me in soberness
as I'm losing you.

ROOM ENOUGH

You once told me I'd never be
the most beautiful woman in the room, so what
nakedness of my flaws were pancaked opaque
enough to trick you so close? So what
if I'm always the palest in the crowd, my lips hike
above the gum line when I laugh or if tired
skirts my eyes like a bustle? Maybe,

for you,

I'm the last one here in this echoing chamber.
The others left,
halted out of their youth in a daze, got comfortable
in wilting skin, found solace in lard and pants
with too much give. Every woman wants
a room of her own, one with a view—a place
where the undisclosed roam free and the knocks
come as soft flurries at the thick door like children
spilling over with cheap Halloween sugar
and rolled like caterpillars into fall-apart costumes.

THE SICKEST WAYS

I find myself pleasing
in the sickest ways,
how my clavicle rides eager
over my breasts like armor.
How my veins corset forearms,
crisscrossed and clumsy. And the way
I love you stupid still
after all the long jumps,
the almost giving ups and mistakes
as big as nightmares. There's something
awe-striking in the magnitude
not even this cloying illness can burst.

THE WEIRD FORK

We had that one weird fork, bigger
than the rest with a bent prong
that scraped my incisor when I slipped
guilt between my lips. Neither of us
could remember where it came from,
where its comrades marched off to
or what hardships caused the bend.
But I couldn't throw it out—it lasted
even after we overspent on overpriced
designer utensils and swapped
the plastic shelving units for oak
casings. It demanded attention
in its otherness, its faults, the utter
monstrosity of its being.

MORNING PASTRIES

You smell like bread in the mornings, something
I want to curl into, all rising yeast and cardamom
notes. It's in the early hours when you're sweetest,
unable to open both eyes and black ribbons of hair
leave sacrificial coils on white sheets. Your heat bakes
into the blankets like an oven—that's why
I come back after my tea, after the lemon squeezes,
after the first writings pour from my fingertips.
In tangled sheets and waves of duvets,
I ride the surf into the morning sun with you,
tucked safe as a child in your arms.

IN DEPENDENCE

Women, we give 'til it's gone, our total
selves, every last scrap of love and crumb
of affection. I didn't let you swallow me whole,
I begged for it, stuffed it down your throat,
clogged your windpipes and ballooned
your belly with the utter everything of Me. Women,

we think it's a gift—that a sacrifice means more
the harder we suffer for it. With you,
I kept dishing it up, doling it out in heaping
spoonfuls and forkfuls of More, praying
your taste buds would adapt to my flavor,
that the addictive threads which slide through my veins
would sidle up to your limbic system exposed
and unashamed. Did it work, my pushes of gluttony
and selfish selflessness of it all? Do you crave
Me like I always have you, from the moment
you hit my papillae like rich chocolate, decadent
and addictive in the dopamine rush?

TOTEM OF YOU

I've built a totem of you, hand carved
devotion—it filled my fingers with splinters,
my palms with gummy sap in the working wood

of adoring you. That weekend at the redwoods,
I slipped a piece of the Immortal Tree
into my denim. It's carried on a thousand years,
through the fires, the floods, bolts
of lightning and hungry loggers. It was like us,
solid through the storms, indifferent
to the whispers, stoic through the rough times.
Afterward, the guilt soaked in, heavy, fatty,
and heady as rum cake. I buried the sacrifice
in the garden, gave it back to the Earth,
begged forgiveness of the Universe. But for you—

your totem is made of the branches of my mind,
the trunk of my body, the leaves of my heart.
Natives say the real beauty of the totem
is in the decay, the slow deterioration, the quiet
death we accept in comfortable silence. Not us,

for us the carvings will stay sharp, the etchings
forever unmoved. I built this monument with my
everything,
a colloquy to where we've been
and the unshakeable of millenniums to come.

TABLE D'HÔTE

Everything would be easier had I never found you,
but who wants a simple life? Give me the hard stuff,
the twists that leave us lurching and introversions
that make hearts gush. I see the settling
all around me—comforts others cling
to like pilled blankets. I watch their waists
expand, habits stick like sloshed batter
on hot stovetops. And it's devastating,
that slow shuffle back to the earth. Their heads
tuck down into heavy, invisible feedbags
as the fattening season drones on, but we,
we've carried on. The two of us,

we carry on.

WHAT'S LEFT BEHIND

You outgrow places just like clothes,
like perfumes, like people. I was done here, we
were done here. This battleground we'd leveled,
truces had been made, a few mines lost in the field,
but, hey,
peace had been held long enough
to call it a victory of sorts. Let's move on,
leave the bad stuff behind. The tear-blood nights,
the shattered glass frames, the years
of back and forth. I've never been scared
of a clean slate—it's breathtaking
in its emptiness. I don't care about the treasures
forgotten with the forlorn, mixed and mangled
like a kid's idea of a cocktail. The best of things
we'll carry with us, folded into memories
and puffing up our hearts when the days ahead
get too heavy to hold. And the worst days?
We'll let them go, stride right over them
like sticky bar floors in the morning light,
disgusted at what happened and promising
through razor migraines and furry tongues
we won't be so idiotic to do it all again.

MAE UN TANG IN YOGA PANTS

I see the men who look at me, the young ones,
the white ones, the boys whose muscles
have barely swollen past puberty. They're the ones
who were sharpened like knives to think
me beautiful. They whistle from their cars, demand,
Show me your tits! as they stoop in bus stops. I tell them,
You could be my child, as I glide by, all tiny
thighs and wasp's waist that seems snappable
as an apple core in their grabbing, greedy hands.
They look at me

like the Koreans do at fish stews—gluttonous
for the fragile bones poking out dangerously
from pale flesh. They see me as something fit
for their mouths, enjoyed in gulps
and forgotten the moment it's swallowed.
I'm not beautiful,

not to them—not in their barbarous parts, the inky
spots pushed down like bad dreams. I'm what they're told
is desirable, what they're supposed to like—
a human substitute for wooden hangers. This,

it isn't beauty. It's a stench that pulses outward
into the streets, intoxicating in the severity
and shockingly eye-catching in the rot.

AMPUTATION SCARE ONE: THE BRONX

They called me Jennifer Cole and I was scared
to die with the wrong name—
who would find me? Bother
to dig through the morgue
for the sickest little candy piece? Yet,

I didn't correct them. Trained my brain
to respond to *Jennifers*, getting full
on hope that if nobody
could find me, maybe that went
for the insurance people, too.

That's not how it works. I left
New York's grimy hospital stuck
like a nana's embroidery, heavy
with bills and crossed-fingered
lucky starred that I still

had all my limbs to love you.

LOVELY IN THE STRANGE

There are times I feel I don't know you
at all, just

as it should be. The words in your head
roll in an alien language, all *Bh* and *Kh*,
aspirations my tongue refuses to contort
into creation like some bizarre circus of the mouth. Your
                                                    dreams
tangle like tipsy lovers in a culture, history, place
I'll never understand, worlds away
from my own. I don't want to know you,
not every crevice,
not every space. Let the others breed
into dullness and contempt, our crashes are made up
of a perfect Venn diagram, rich
in mystery and lovely in the strange.

THE OTHER SIDE

Call this a love letter, call it
Our Story,
unlike anyone else's, but with threads
and adornments from the Great
Ones—the star-crossed fables, the fairy tales
we craved and gobbled down as greedy
little beasts in our parents' arms. Call this
what shouldn't have been, all hurdles
and bounds through flaming hoops,
seasoned with heartbreaks and flavored
with blindfolded leaps. There are all kinds
of names for what we've done, for who
we are and where we've been.
Call it a freak accident, a liquored up
lurch into just the right nook
of just the right place. This
is called finding the great stuff
and having the thick tenacity
to hold on knuckle-white
through all the blinding explosions.

_ _ _ _ _ _ **UP**

Stupid, the lot of us, signing
up for facial
abuse shots or busking
for validation in bars—it's all
the same. I never realized
my mother's judgment slid
like disease through
the umbilical cord
or that hate and anorexia
could be genetic.
What do I care
how long my hair grows
or if my sharpened nails
would make me a terrible
lesbian? We're ridiculous,
laughable, no wonder
we're so thankful for the blackouts.

TRY THIS ON

I put on weight slowly, carefully,
contrived. It was pure
muscle, all Does this curve
make me look fat? and
Does this vein make me look jacked?
I eased into it, tried it on,
took it back off then slipped
into it again. It was odd, feeling
Normal. Not all size zeroes
fit anymore. Sometimes
my thighs kiss each other, skeletons
no longer stare back from mirrors.
And I miss them
at times, those ghosts, the bony
collar bones and knocking knees
so beautiful in the haunting.

ORYGUN

When I find myself missing
Wild, I walk for hours through the wet-
lands til my hips grind to dust
and the mud suckles my feet.
This is what I'll miss
when another city swallows me whole.
The deer hooves in the deep,
throaty frogs with lustful lines,
marionberries sprawling fat
and frenzied. So let yourself
be Wild. Suck the cold air deep,
rattle it around your lungs
and fog up your insides.
How blessed are we born
into the Oregon green,
how lucky we are to carry
her *ferality* in our bones.

FRUITION

Daily, he brings a too-hard
apple to the French doors. Together,
we've watched them ripen, the green
drip from the roundness,
give way to the red. I don't know

if he's asking permission,
for my blessing, or simply
showing off how goddamned gorgeous
today's find was. *That looks*
like a good one, I tell him.

Daily. And my voice breaks
the silence like thunder. Daily,

he brings an offering
to my doorstep, black eyes shining
with no fear threads.
That's a good one, I tell him,
my words chasing him
with vicious teeth
up the dying, bowing tree.

STILL

Yes, I love you something
stupid still (so, please
stop asking). I can't say why,
there aren't new epiphanies
each day. It's the same
keeping on reasons as always—straight
from the beginning.
You don't remember all the everythings
that drew me close. The
You wear a wicked grin and hand
feedings on makeshift tables.
Those are the whys and they build,
stack upon one another like scaffolding,
like us, like how we knew,
like stubborn children we would get
exactly what we wanted.

NEGOTIATIONS

I made my bed, I ate the sprouts
now give me something special. I've downed
the pills, flossed my teeth waiting
for incredible. The lies I told
were strong and thick, impossible
to unravel. So pinch my cheek
and pull me close, I worked
dogged for forever.

LIKE THE SUN

You still ask me what I see in you, I keep
asking how many books I need to write
to tell you. Knowing, we stomped
our feet into concrete
and stopped our life
from spinning. Like the sun,
the dervishes dance 'round us
while we stay free. Permanent,
at the center of it all.

WRITING

I always say this is the last one, but that's
when I'm empty. When I just got it good—
it's easy then. To act like I've had my fill,
like the craving won't come again, like
I won't say *Okay just once more*, spill
my innards all over. Weave my fingers
through the guts and intestines, spread
out my insides for the world to pick apart.

DRESSED

I wear scars like others wear scarves—
pretty embellishments and pops
of color—like women slip into little
black dresses to flash their pumped
up décolletage, as men pull up their good
worn jeans, tight in the thighs
to peacock the lines drawn sharp with deadlifts.
For me,
my scars are the echoes of passion,
the trimmings of cancers hand cut
for high fashion. They're the accessories
of eating disorders, the pleats and embroidery
of bad plastic surgery, the finishing touches
from the glass shards, jagged ruching,
through curious young flesh.
I wear my scars like you wear your staples,
confident in their permanence and not anywhere able
to care what *they* think. Are the keloids
less appeasing than this season's
heel height? The jagged lines less appealing
when I've ruched up from too slight? I'm draped
in a wardrobe designed just for me, created
by a force beyond the runway, and tailored
to fit like a couture wedding dress, no *prêt à porter*,
cheap knockoffs for the masses. It's a style
beyond what others may choose, but right from the start
it was magnificent—and radiant to you.

JUXTAPOSED IN EIGHT SECONDS

Bareback, we expect them to go crazy,
vigorous kicking legs and shining teeth. The cowboys,
they ride from the chutes like prisoners rushing
razor fences. They don't care
about the bruises, the cuts, the odds of death
or ruined bodies. But this stallion, he stumbled
from the cage blind to the false freedoms
of the fields, sticking close as glue
to the iron fences and stadium. *Climb me up
to heaven*, his help-me eyes sang like hallelujah
as he clawed his hooves along the metal bars
that rang like harmony for the roaring crowds.
We sat where we always did, cooking
beneath the Pendleton sun, sheer trots
from the anxious things. And when that horse,
he could rise no higher, fell backwards
like a sequoia timbering in the forest,
there was paralysis in the stands. Chapped legs
splayed lifeless beneath the withers—a garnish
to the massive croup. Ride that young cowboy,
frantic stallion, his bones seemingly as hollow
as a bird's, that he might fly away as you roll
over his stillness. Crushing fibulas, tibias, young body
smashed like a dropped tumbler in the dust.

THE TEMPORARY NATURE OF BEING

Bedded down in the woods,
the houses rest on stilts, dangerous,
dangling like sleeping children
on top bunks. We tiptoe like gluttons
across the Cascadia faults, as if
the sweets stuffed in cupboards
and ice cream cradled in freezers are fair
trade for our lives. The experts call us
woefully unprepared as we bow, tangled
heads over sugary cereal, the morning
news unable to shock. Tsunamis overseas,
floods on the east coast—we're so sure
nothing can touch us here, not in the Wild
West, never where gold rushes raged
or martinis were conceived in haste. Forest hugs
me close, the occasional sharp thorny fingernails
tracing taut calves or hoggish spider webs
kissing my face. One day,
soon,
it will all come crashing down: The West
Hills homes indie bands made famous,
the teetering decks like behemoths,
foolish and feeble scarecrows in the sky.

EMERGENCY PREPAREDNESS

I've learned to roll through your storms
like a Kansan figures out real quick

bathtubs usually stay put in a twister.
For you I hung on

to the rusted pipes,
the gurgling sounds, the cool slickness
of the underbelly. Our years showed me
to wait out the quiet, bear down hard
and not scramble to drown the silence
just because.
I memorized your moods—
unspoken languages are the easiest,
most terrible to unravel. Now,
I realize when you chop up my pet names
uneven and rough into senseless Hindi
you're happy, ripping at the seams with smiles
and spilling over with touches. When you're hungry,
your skin needs a drink first, lapping up lukewarm
shower rain and soap. And when you don't want to speak,
I can't make you. I shouldn't even try. I know
how to weather the seasons, how to not get soaked
in the downpour and where my secret
umbrellas of strength are kept, bundled tight
and ready to burst open with the slightest push.

PILOT'S LOG: DAY 23

When I was learning to fly, he killed
the engine. Said, *You don't need power*
to stay here. And he was right,
but the silence,
the silence is maddening.
In the quiet your heart blunders
like a drunk against ear drums. Buttons
press aching into pelvis, you notice
how much bigger your thighs
are than his. This

is so amazingly stupid, and radio
static is syrup-
thick while tiny homes below
beg like scared children for you
to come crashing back down.

THE ART OF PATIENCE

From you I learned the art of waiting, the art
of patience. I thought I knew quiet,
drenched myself in it as a child, wore
it like a puffy coat well into adulthood—
when quiet breaks down, you can bury yourself
in layers of fat and bad skin.
But when that sloughed off I was left
with nothing. No quiet,
no buffer, nothing to keep me safe
from the shark-like assaults
of the world. You showed me
what it means to wait. To not speak
just to soften awkwardness, not demand
answers when they're as undeveloped
as the embryos I flushed from my body,
never regretted remnants from the lost years.
You taught me the beauty of closed lips,
the power of reticence and how to command,
thundering like a lion with my eyes.

AGING

Am I strange that getting old fits
me like a good suit, goes down
like a buttery oyster—just two chews
to perfection? I wear these new lines
like the sweater that smells of you, comfortable
in the cloying, fragile in the flailing. My god,
who would want to do their twenties
again, the teenage years steeped in angst
or childhoods where traumas are
big as whales and our parents acerbic
gods? Me, I barely survived the first
time around that macabre carousel, just look
at these battle scars: The first threads
of silver, the laugh lines running heavy,
and the crow's feet cawing with lungs
of steel echoing over weathered tombstones.

ORYGUN

AUTHOR

Jessica Tyner Mehta is an award-winning poet, novelist and writer. A native Oregonian and member of the Cherokee Nation, her work has been published in over 50 magazines and journals around the world and was nominated for a Pushcart Prize. Jessica has lived in, and written  extensively about, the UK, South Korea and Costa Rica but continues to return to "Orygun" for her steadfast inspiration. She has been a featured reader at numerous literary events including India's International Poetry Festival (New Delhi), Wordstock (Portland, Ore.), the International Women's Writing Guild Summer Conference (Allentown, Penn.), and Berl's Poetry Bookshop (Brooklyn). Jessica also reads and performs her work as a "poetry whore" with the international Poetry Brothel series.

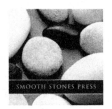

CPSIA information can be obtained at www.ICGtesting.com
Printed in the USA
BVOW06*2142220916

462878BV00005B/3/P